TECHNOLOGY TOPICS

SHIPS and SHIPWRECKS

Steve Blackman

illustrated by **Jeremy Pyke**
photography by **Martyn Chillmaid**

WATTS BOOKS
London • New York • Sydney

© Watts Books 1993

Watts Books
96 Leonard Street
London
EC2A 4RH

Franklin Watts Australia
14 Mars Road
Lane Cove
NSW 2066

UK ISBN: 0 7496 1241 X
10 9 8 7 6 5 4 3 2 1
Dewey Decimal Classification 623.8

Series Editor: Hazel Poole
Editor: Chris Oxlade
Designer: Glynn Pickerill
Illustrator: Jeremy Pyke
Design Production: The R & B Partnership
Cover design and artwork: Mike Davis
Photography: Martyn Chillmaid
Consultant: Rowland Penfold

A CIP catalogue record for this book is
available from the British Library

Printed in the United Kingdom

CONTENTS

All Kinds of Craft 4

The Shape of Hulls 6

Shipwrecks Around the World 8

Shipwreck File 10

The *Titanic* 12

Raising the Wreck 14

Self-righting Vessels 16

Make a Self-righting Craft 18

Safety on Board 20

Make a Model Lifebelt 22

Sailing Ships 24

Make a Sailing Boat 26

Sailing Through the Ages 28

Glossary 30

Resources 31

Index 32

ALL KINDS OF CRAFT

Oil tankers (right) are specially designed to carry thousands of tonnes of oil around the world. They are among the biggest ships in the world. Some oil tankers are so long that the crew have to use bicycles or mopeds to get around on deck. In poor visibility the crew cannot see the bow from the bridge!

The *Sea Cat* (below) is a catamaran. It has a top speed of 80 kilometres per hour – twice as fast as a normal ferry. It can carry 80 cars and 450 passengers. Its catamaran hull is shaped to produce a hydrofoil lifting effect.

Vehicle ferries (left) are known as roll-on, roll-off ships (ro-ro for short) because the vehicles are driven in and out of the hold. They can carry cars, lorries and coaches in the lower decks and there are comfortable lounges for passengers on the upper decks.

Submarines (below) are built for underwater travel. They are able to dive and resurface quickly. During World War II, submarines proved to be a deadly weapon. Today, nuclear-powered submarines can stay submerged for many months, until supplies run out.

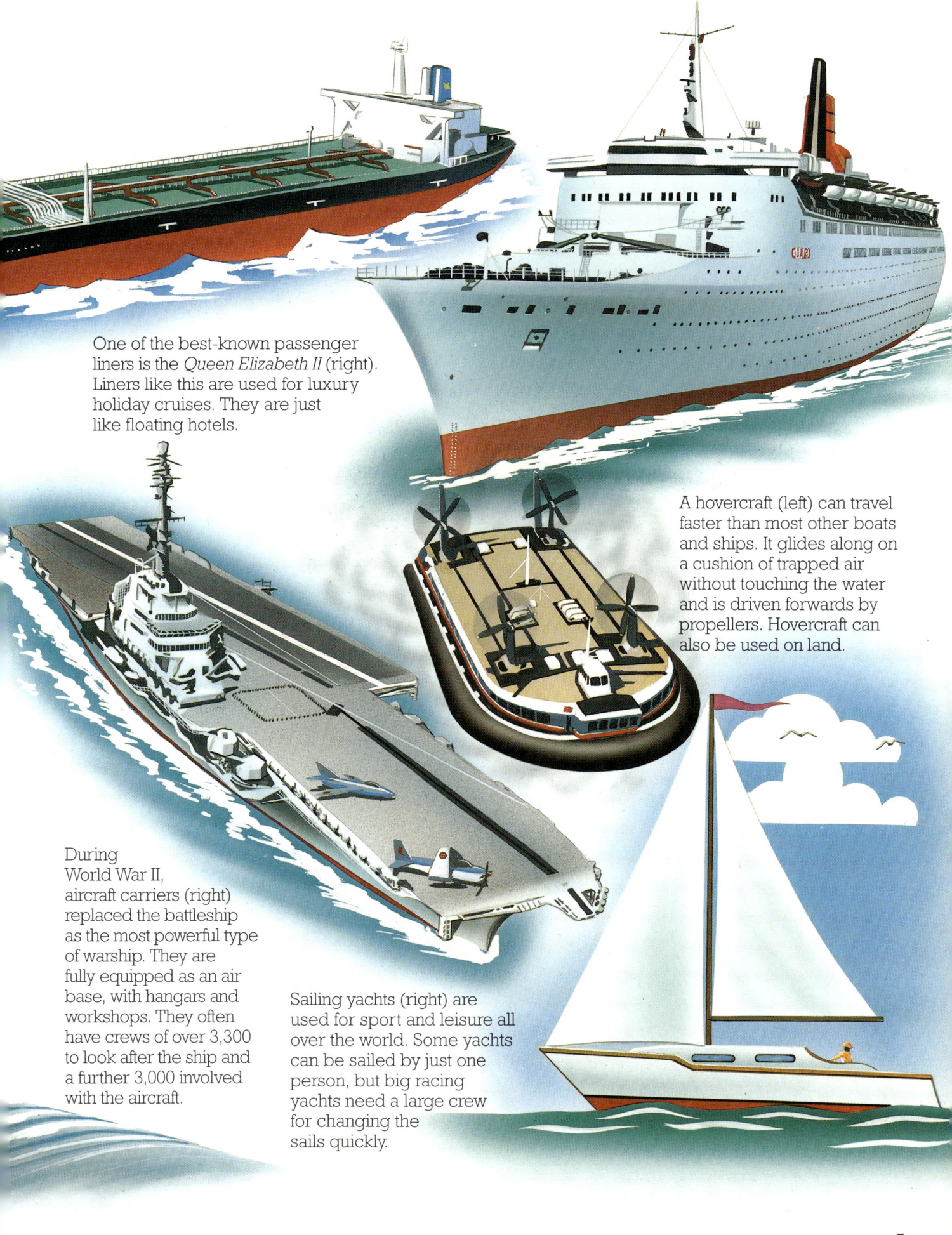

One of the best-known passenger liners is the *Queen Elizabeth II* (right). Liners like this are used for luxury holiday cruises. They are just like floating hotels.

A hovercraft (left) can travel faster than most other boats and ships. It glides along on a cushion of trapped air without touching the water and is driven forwards by propellers. Hovercraft can also be used on land.

During World War II, aircraft carriers (right) replaced the battleship as the most powerful type of warship. They are fully equipped as an air base, with hangars and workshops. They often have crews of over 3,300 to look after the ship and a further 3,000 involved with the aircraft.

Sailing yachts (right) are used for sport and leisure all over the world. Some yachts can be sailed by just one person, but big racing yachts need a large crew for changing the sails quickly.

THE SHAPE OF HULLS

The hull is the main part of any ship. It forms the body of the ship and is the part that touches the water.

The weight of a ship pushes the hull down into the water. The hull then takes up room in the water. This is called displacement. As this happens, the water around the hull pushes the hull upwards. This force is called upthrust. The more water the hull displaces, the greater the upthrust. A ship sinks into the water, displacing more and more water, until the upthrust is great enough to support its weight. Then it floats.

The shape of a ship's hull depends on the job the ship is designed to do:

● A fast racing yacht has a sleek, streamlined hull so that it can cut through the water easily.

● A fast speedboat has a shallow, v-shaped hull that lets it skim quickly over the water.

● Ferries that operate in shallow waters have wide hulls so that they do not sink too deeply into the water.

Some ships have a keel. This is like a backbone running along the bottom of the hull. A yacht has a heavy keel which extends down into the water. This helps to keep it stable and stop it drifting when the wind is blowing from the side.

Floating and sinking

You may need:
- a ball of Plasticine
- a bowl of water
- card
- gloss paint (any colour)
- scissors
- ruler
- sticky tape
- glue

1 Roll the Plasticine into a firm ball and put it into the bowl of water. Does it float?

The ball sinks because it does not displace enough water for the upthrust to equal its weight. The hull shape displaces more water, and so there is enough upthrust to support it.

2 Mould the Plasticine into a simple hull shape. Make sure that there are no holes in it. Does your hull shape float?

Put coins into your hull one by one. Watch what happens. Can you explain it?

3 Make a box-shaped hull from the card.

4 Paint the hull with gloss paint to make it waterproof. Leave it to dry.

Does the hull float?
Will it carry a load?
How easily does it move through the water?

5 Make a keel from card and fix it to the hull. Paint it with gloss paint.

Try the tests again. Are the results the same?

6 Add a pointed bow to the hull to make it a more streamlined shape. Now paint it.

Try the tests again. What difference does the streamlined hull make?

7 Make a completely new hull. This time, make the bow, keel and hull in one piece.

Can you find ways of improving the shape even more.

SHIPWRECKS
AROUND THE WORLD

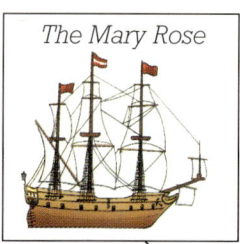
The Mary Rose

The Amsterdam

The Hope

Amoco Cadiz

The Titanic

The Bismarck

The Concepcion

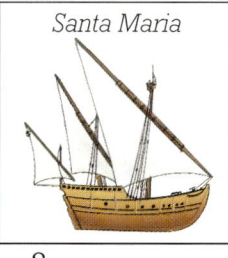
Santa Maria

North America

Atlantic Ocean

Equator

South America

SHIPWRECK FILE

ENGLISH CHANNEL

The *Mary Rose* was Henry VIII's flagship and the pride of the English navy. On 19 July 1545, she was in the Solent on the south coast of England, when she was hit by a gust of wind. She leaned over, water poured in through her gun ports, and she sank. The wreck of the *Mary Rose* was raised from the seabed in 1982.

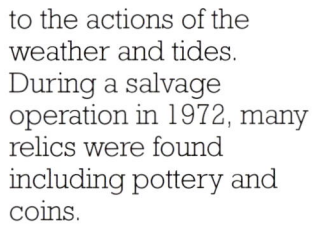

On 16 January 1749 the *Hope,* a Dutch ship, was blown off course in bad weather and was washed up on the coast of Dorset in southern England. Luckily, the masts fell towards the shore and the crew scrambled to safety. The *Hope* was carrying a cargo of gold and silver bullion worth £50,000.

On 16 March 1978, the *Amoco Cadiz* smashed into rocks off the coast of Brittany in France. More than a quarter of a million tonnes of oil poured into the sea. The Brittany coastline was badly polluted.

The Dutch ship *Amsterdam* lost her rudder while on a voyage in 1749. She was washed ashore on the coast of England and gradually fell apart due to the actions of the weather and tides. During a salvage operation in 1972, many relics were found including pottery and coins.

THE ATLANTIC OCEAN

The German battleship *Bismarck* sank on 27 May 1941 after a great sea battle with British warships. As it sank, the huge gun turrets fell off and hit the seabed before the rest of the ship. The wreck of the *Bismarck* was found by Dr Robert Ballard. It lies 400 kilometres off the coast of France, where the sea is 4,760 metres deep. Its exact position is kept secret because it is now a memorial to the people who died on board.

The famous *Titanic* was a passenger liner which sank in 1912. You can find out all about her on page 12.

THE CARIBBEAN

The *Santa Maria* was Christopher Columbus' flagship. On 24 December 1492, she began to drift while at anchor. The cabin boy on watch realised too late what was happening and the *Santa Maria* collided

with the beach. She was too badly damaged to be repaired. Nothing remains of the wreck so nobody knows exactly where the accident happened.

The *Concepcion* was a Spanish treasure ship. She was destroyed in storms near the Dominican Republic while sailing back to Spain with a cargo of gold and silver coins. The wreck was discovered in the 1970s, and much of the treasure is on display in the museum in Santo Domingo in the Dominican Republic. Some of the coins were sold to raise money so that other wrecks could be explored.

THE INDIAN OCEAN

In 1977, marine archaeologists discovered the remains of a hull near Mombasa on the east coast of Africa. It was made from teak and was part of a Portuguese frigate, the *Santo Antonio de Tanna,* built in 1681 to protect Portuguese trading ships in the Indian Ocean.

On 26 February 1852, the *Birkenhead,* a troop-ship carrying 624 people, hit a submerged rock just off the coast of South Africa. She sank in under 25 minutes and as the ship had only eight lifeboats, only 193 people survived.

THE YELLOW SEA

The wreck of a 14th-century Chinese merchant ship was found near Sinan, on the south-west coast of Korea, in 1975. It is thought that the ship was wrecked in a storm while on its way to Japan. About 12,000 objects have been recovered from the wreck.

THE MEDITERRANEAN SEA

Marine archaeologists found the wreck of a Greek merchant ship near Kyrenia, in Cyprus. The ship was built in the 4th century BC and was carrying over 400 amphoras (pottery jars) full of almonds. There were also some millstones, which were probably used as ballast.

In 1980, the wreck of a Roman ship was found just off Puerto de la Selva in Spain. It was a merchant ship used in the Mediterranean Sea in the 1st century BC. Among other things, some human hair was found on board.

Did You Know ...
... the oldest shipwreck ever found was discovered off the Turkish coast at Ulu Burun? It was of a merchant ship more than 3,400 years old. The objects found included swords, pottery, jewellery, glassware and gold. They give an idea of the type of things that were being traded by people in the Mediterranean Sea at that time.

THE TITANIC

On 10 April 1912, the *Titanic* sailed from Southampton on her maiden voyage across the North Atlantic. The 2,224 passengers on board were looking forward to enjoying the best accommodation, food and entertainment on the luxury liner. The ship catered for First, Second and Third Class passengers in the most luxurious surroundings. There was even a swimming pool and gymnasium on board.

The *Titanic* was also fitted with safety features which were supposed to make her unsinkable. Nobody could have predicted the tragedy that was about to happen.

When the *Titanic* was built, she was the biggest ocean liner in the world. She was 269 metres long, 28 metres wide, and weighed over 46,000 tonnes. She had eight decks and was as high as an 11-storey building. Fifty thousand men took two years to build her and she was launched in Belfast, Northern Ireland, on 31 May 1911.

ON SUNDAY 14 April, the temperature dropped suddenly. The wireless operator received a warning of icebergs. Surprisingly, the *Titanic* continued to race on at full speed.

At 11.29 pm, the forward look-out saw a large dark shape. Immediately, he rang the alarm bell three times and reported "Iceberg dead ahead!"

All efforts to steer the liner away were hopeless. Within 10 seconds, the iceberg had ripped into the starboard side of the ship, and the sea poured in.

The *Titanic* was built with 16 watertight compartments. The ship's designers believed that up to five of them could be flooded without the ship being in danger. The iceberg had holed six, and water overflowed into the other compartments, one by one, until the ship sank.

The order was given to abandon ship – women and children first because there were not enough lifeboats for everybody. The loaded lifeboats were lowered while husbands, fathers and crew members watched calmly. The orchestra continued to play – even as the ship went under.

It was soon after 2 am on Monday 15 April when the *Titanic* sank. It was less than three hours since she hit the iceberg. As the *Titanic* sank, she broke in half between her third and fourth funnels. Other ships in the area picked up 711 survivors. A total of 1513 lives were lost.

Shipwreck Hunting

In September 1985, Dr Robert Ballard and his team of American and French scientists found the wreck of the *Titanic*. It was five kilometres below the surface. They used the very latest technology, including a new sonar designed especially for scanning the seabed.

A deep-sea robot submarine equipped with underwater cameras took photographs. It was the world's first glimpse of the *Titanic* for more than 70 years.

Shipwreck hunting can be a profitable business, especially when treasure is found. However, it was decided to leave the *Titanic* undisturbed as a memorial to the people who died.

RAISING THE WRECK

You may need:

- a small plastic or wooden boat (or the model hulls you have already made)
- a fish tank or washing-up bowl
- some weights
- thin, stiff wire
- a piece of wooden broom handle
- a piece of plastic pipe
- lengths of thin wood
- string
- plastic bottles
- balloons
- a flexible tube
- a bicycle pump
- strong magnets
- strong, waterproof sticky tape
- several corks

Use some of the equipment to create a wreck under water. You may need to add weights to your boat to make it sink.

Now try some of these ways of raising your wreck.

1 Make a winch which stands over the water. Put the loops around the wreck and winch it up.

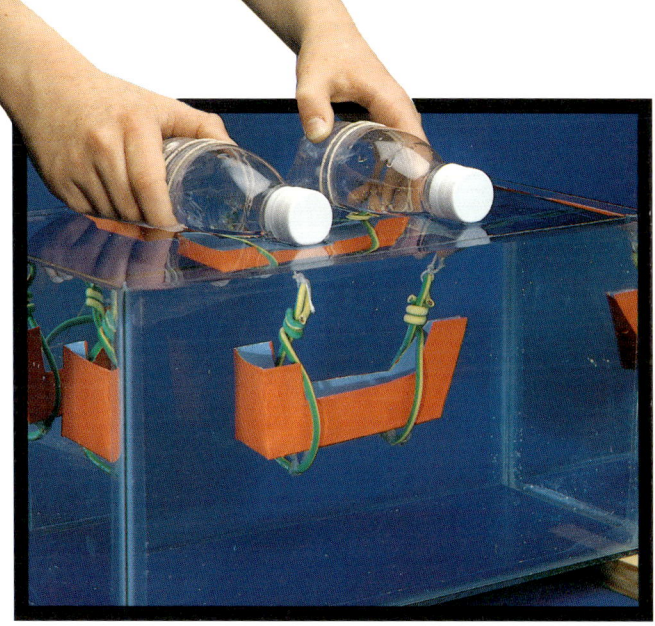

2 Use two plastic bottles as a floating winch. Put the loops around the wreck and winch it up by turning the bottles.

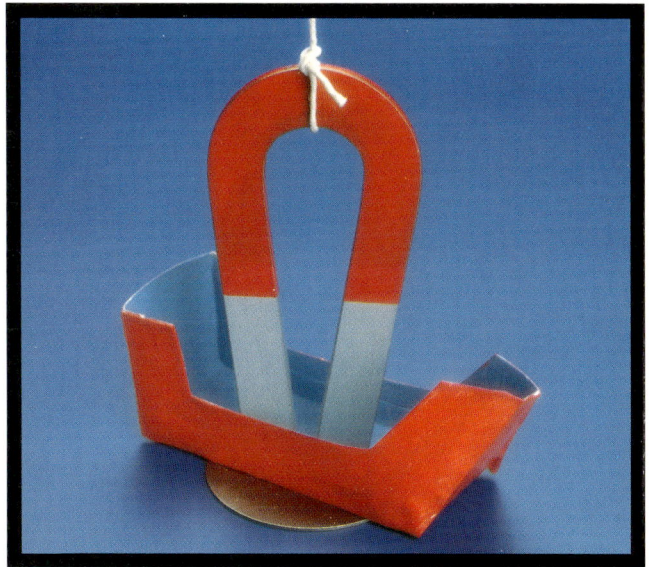

4 Attach a strong magnet to the wreck. Put another magnet on to your winch. Winch up the wreck.

Can you think of any other methods of raising the wreck?
How would you get your wreck to the shore?

Rules
Follow these rules while you are trying to raise your wreck.
* Don't touch the wreck with your hands.
* Don't take the water out of the tank.
* Don't move the tank in any way.

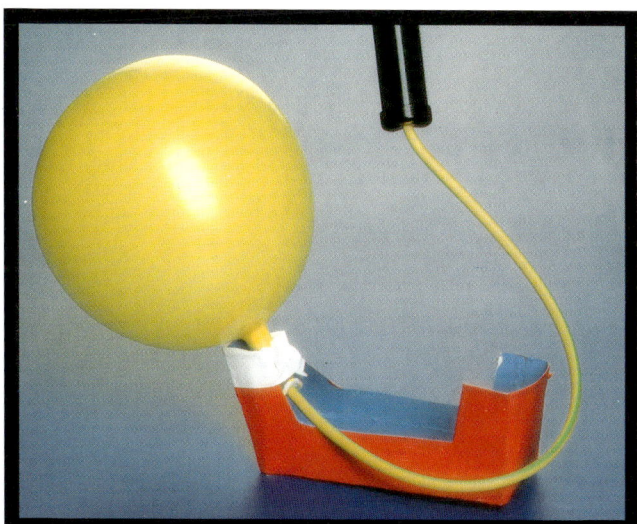

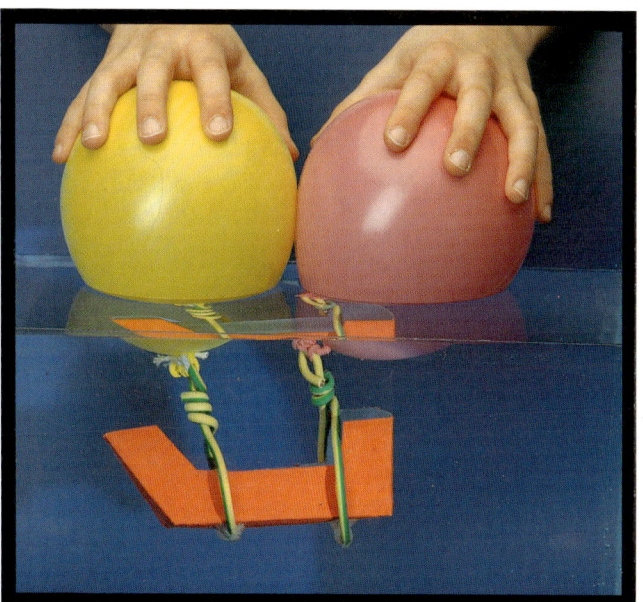

3 Attach balloons to the wreck and inflate them with the pump and tube.

Did You Know ...
... the wreck of the *Mary Rose* was discovered in 1966? It had laid underwater since it sank in 1545. Over the next 16 years it was carefully excavated and mapped. Marine archaeologists found many artifacts which have helped them learn about life in the 16th century. The *Mary Rose* was raised on 11 October 1982. It was encased in a steel frame and lifted using a giant floating crane.

SELF-RIGHTING VESSELS

Designers and builders have spent many years trying to build an unsinkable vessel. The owners of the *Titanic* thought it was unsinkable because of its special watertight compartments. When we call a vessel unsinkable, we are really saying that it would not sink under "normal" sailing conditions. Very strong winds can create waves big enough to capsize ships and boats. Self-righting vessels are designed to turn back up the right way by themselves. The best-known type of self-righting vessel is the lifeboat. Some navy ships and oil-rig support ships are also self-righting.

Making a boat self-righting

The engine of a lifeboat is placed as deep in the hull as possible. This keeps the boat's weight low down and so makes it more stable. A lifeboat is also completely watertight. All the joints are carefully sealed, the hatches and portholes shut very tightly, trapping air inside the cabin.

Even if it is swamped, a lifeboat cannot sink because of its trapped air. If a lifeboat capsizes, the weight of the engine at the top pushes down and the air in the cabin underneath pushes up. This makes the boat spin back up the right way.

It is vitally important for lifeboats to be self-righting because they can be put to sea in very bad weather when there is a high risk of capsizing.

The first self-righting lifeboats were designed in 1851. The Royal National Lifeboat Institution in the United Kingdom has used them ever since. One of the larger types of lifeboat used around the United Kingdom is called the Tyne Class. It can right itself in about four seconds.

A CANOE IS not really a self-righting vessel, but a canoeist can easily roll back up after a capsize.

The word canoe originates from the Taino Indians of Hispaniola in the Caribbean. The native Americans and Inuit of Canada adapted the canoe for their own use. Modern canoes are fast and highly-manoeuvrable boats, and canoeing is a popular sport.

Make a SELF-RIGHTING CRAFT

The stability of a craft depends on where its centre of gravity is. All objects have a centre of gravity. Try balancing a ruler on your fingertip. Where is the centre of gravity? When the ruler balances perfectly, its centre of gravity is over your finger. The centre of gravity of a ship depends on how the ship is built and where the cargo is. The further down into the hull the centre of gravity is, the more stable the ship is.

You may need:

- a wooden boat shape
- a piece of dowel
- a weight
- balsa wood
- nails
- a table tennis ball
- plastic tape
- a bowl or tank of water

1 Make a basic wooden boat shape with a flat bottom. Carefully fix a mast to it. Make a mark every centimetre along the mast, starting from the bottom. Fix the weight around the mast so that it can slide up and down.

Start with the weight at the bottom of the mast. How stable is the boat in the water? Gradually raise the weight up the mast. What happens to the stability?
What is happening to the centre of gravity? How far up the mast is the weight when the boat capsizes all the time?

2 Make a model boat from balsa wood.

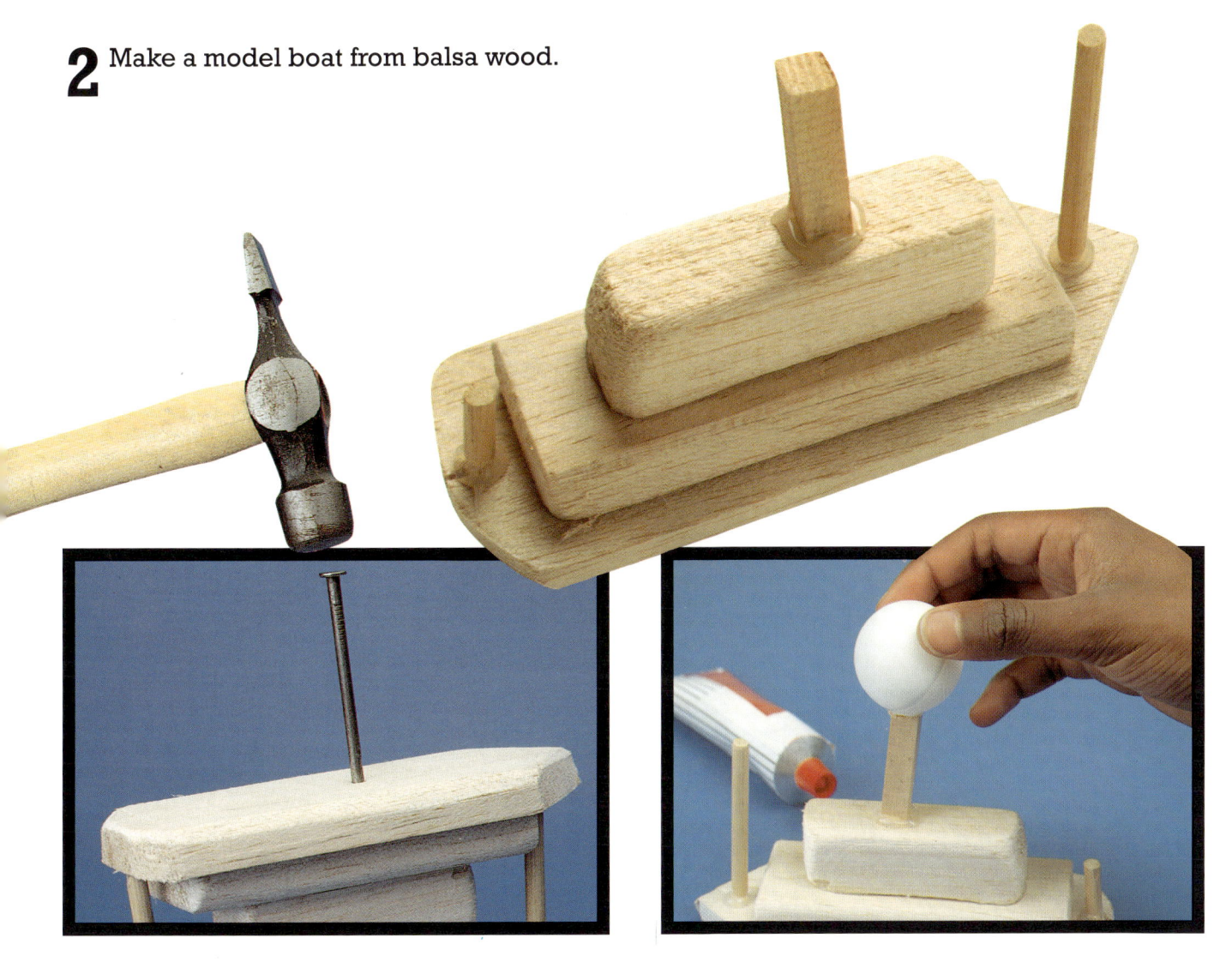

3 Add a nail to the bottom of the boat, directly underneath the funnel. Fix a table-tennis ball to the funnel.

4 When the boat capsizes, it will right itself. Can you alter the boat so that it rights itself more quickly.

Did You Know ...
... on 15 November 1928, 17 lives were lost in a lifeboat disaster?. The lifeboat *Mary Stanford* was sent out from Rye harbour in England to rescue a ship in trouble. The lifeboat was not self-righting and capsized with the loss of all the crew.

SAFETY ON BOARD

Life-rafts and Lifeboats

Life-rafts are another important life-saving device. They inflate automatically when they are launched overboard from a ship. Life-rafts can stay afloat in the roughest sea conditions. The large ones hold as many as 50 people, keeping them warm and dry while they wait to be rescued.

Many larger ships have lifeboats as well as life-rafts. They can be launched quickly in the event of an emergency. Lifeboats are powered by an outboard or inboard motor. They also carry oars just in case!

There are many other smaller items of emergency equipment on board. They include parachute flares, hand-held flares and signalling torches.

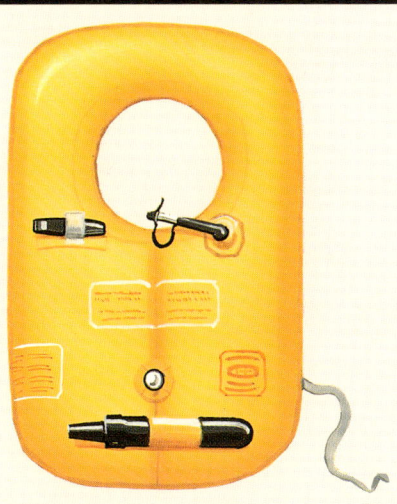

THE LIFE-JACKET IS a safety device which is carried on ships and boats of all sizes.

Early life-jackets were made from panels of cork, or from silky fibres called kapok. Today, they are made from lightweight nylon fabric and are self-inflating. They can be made as part of normal clothing.

On larger ships, such as ferries, life-jackets are spread around the ship and their position is well labelled. Experienced sailors would agree that the life-jacket and the compass are the most important pieces of equipment on board ship.

NAVIGATIONAL AIDS On modern ships, electronic navigational aids are an important part of the safety equipment. On-board computers receive satellite signals and give the position of the ship with pin-point accuracy.

Radar shows the position of other ships, the coastline and other possible hazards. It has a range of about 60 kilometres. Radar is especially important in busy shipping lanes, such as the English Channel.

Sonar equipment sends sound waves down to the seabed and detects echoes. Sonar is used to measure the depth of the water and can also spot underwater obstacles.

Make a Model LIFEBELT

A great deal of research and planning goes into the design of life-saving equipment. It must be the correct size and shape, and above all it must be made with the correct materials. Life-jackets and lifebelts are brightly coloured so that they can be easily seen. They must be waterproof, water-resistant, and of course, buoyant.

To make a model lifebelt

You may need:

- **polystyrene tiles**
- **corks**
- **plastic carrier bags**
- **plastic tape**
- **newspaper**
- **wallpaper paste (fungicide free)**
- **gloss paint**
- **varnish**
- **chicken wire**
- **cord**
- **paper**

IMPORTANT: REMEMBER, THIS IS ONLY A MODEL LIFEBELT, IT CANNOT BE USED TO SAVE LIVES.

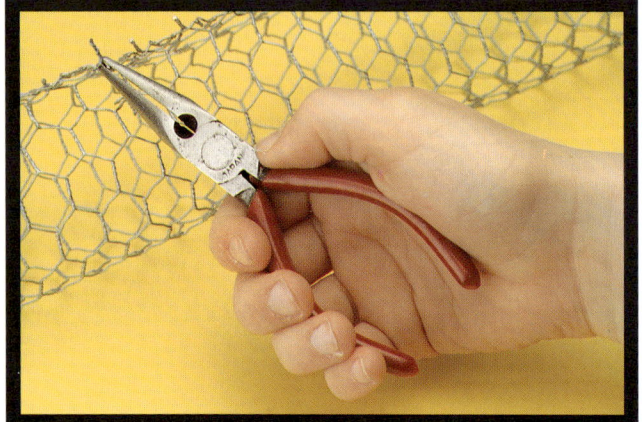

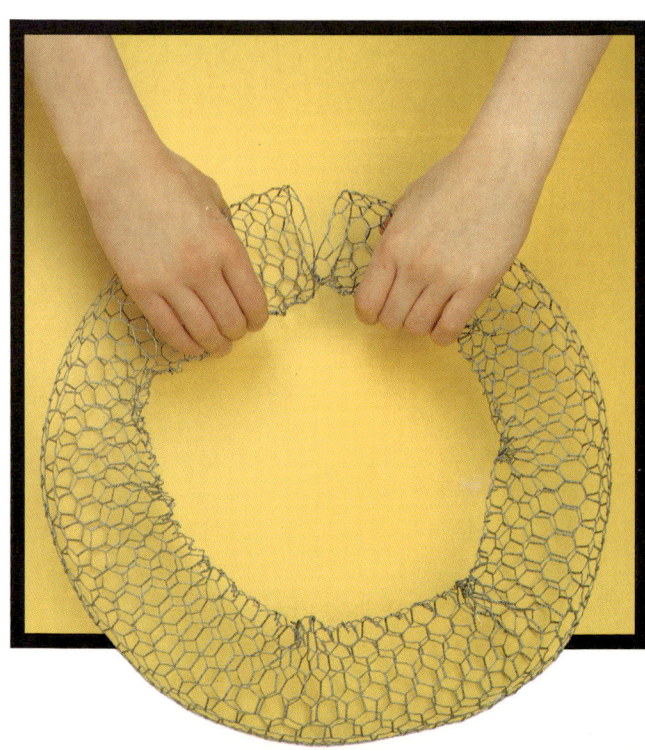

1 Make a cylinder shape about 80cm long from chicken wire. Take care as you do this - chicken wire has sharp points when it is cut. Use a pair of pliers to shape the tube into a circle and to turn back any sharp ends of wire.

22

2 Cover the wire frame with strips of newspaper soaked in wallpaper paste. Build up about six layers, so that the outside is smooth.

3 Add two more layers, but this time use plain paper. Let the paper dry completely. This could take up to a week in a warm room.

4 Paint the model white with red bands. Add a cord and stencil on a ship's name. Finally, add two coats of varnish.

5 Use card to make a housing to store your lifebelt.

Place your lifebelt in the bath. Does it float? Can you improve the design?

Can you make another lifebelt, this time with cork, polystyrene or plastic inside the frame, and no paper cover? What is your most successful design?

Sailing Ships

The first sailing ships had simple square sails. They could only sail along in the same direction as the wind. To get back again, they had to be rowed along. In the Middle Ages, the lateen sail was invented. This meant that ships could sail wherever the crew wanted, no matter where the wind was blowing from.

Luxury sailing ships have computer-controlled sails. Below deck there are comfortable cabins for the passengers. People can still enjoy adventure holidays on older sailing ships.

The Arab dhow has a lateen sail. It is triangular and hangs from a spar, attached to the mast at about 45°. The boat can sail in most directions, except straight into the wind. By steering a zig-zag course, the boat can travel against the wind. This is called tacking. Although modern yachts have a different arrangement of sails, they work in the same way.

Lateen sails were often used together with square sails. There were many different arrangements, many of which are still in use today.

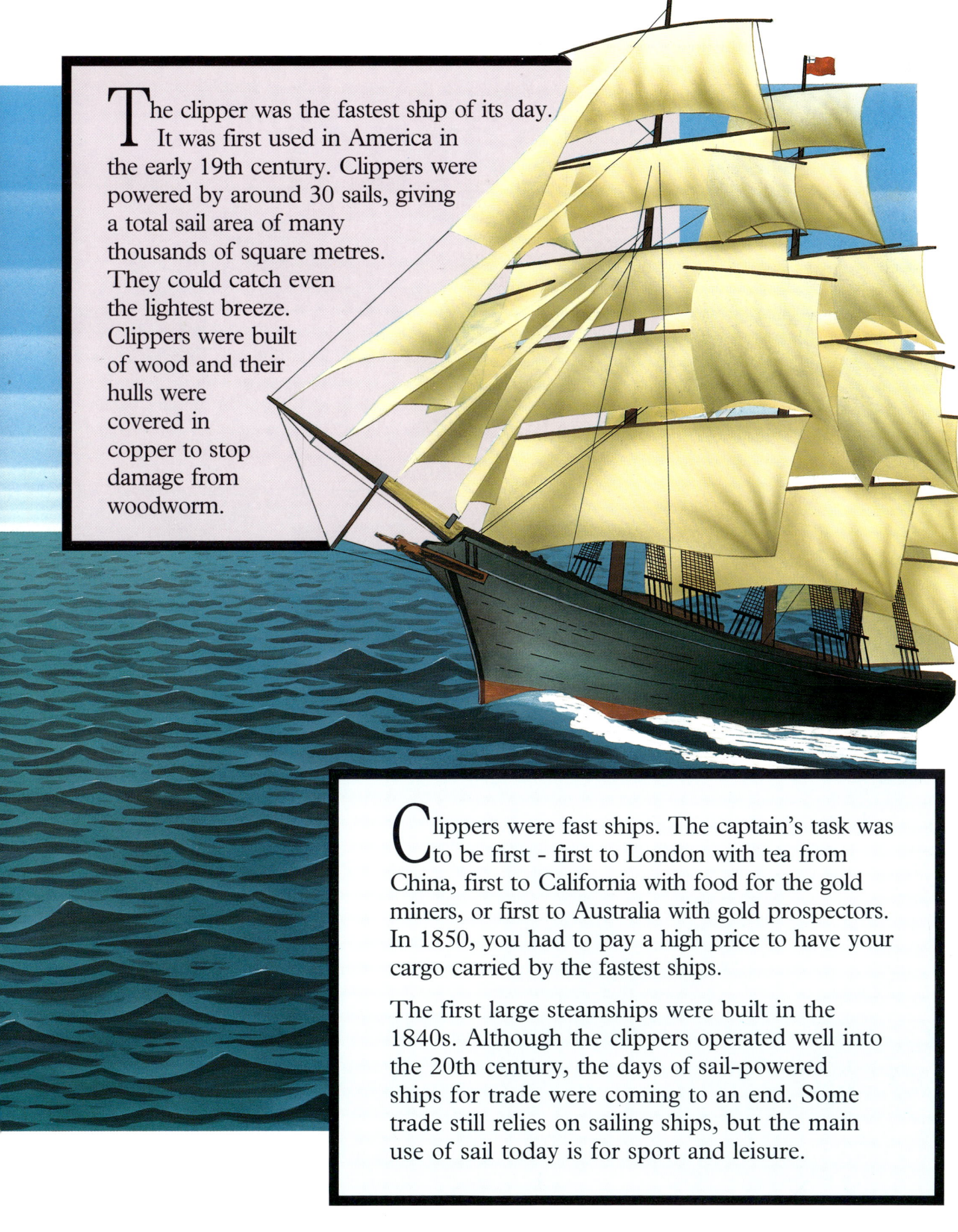

The clipper was the fastest ship of its day. It was first used in America in the early 19th century. Clippers were powered by around 30 sails, giving a total sail area of many thousands of square metres. They could catch even the lightest breeze. Clippers were built of wood and their hulls were covered in copper to stop damage from woodworm.

Clippers were fast ships. The captain's task was to be first - first to London with tea from China, first to California with food for the gold miners, or first to Australia with gold prospectors. In 1850, you had to pay a high price to have your cargo carried by the fastest ships.

The first large steamships were built in the 1840s. Although the clippers operated well into the 20th century, the days of sail-powered ships for trade were coming to an end. Some trade still relies on sailing ships, but the main use of sail today is for sport and leisure.

Make a SAILING BOAT

You may need:
- a block of balsa wood
- a rasp
- sandpaper
- a piece of dowel
- cotton fabric
- gloss paint or varnish
- string
- 2 eye hooks
- glue
- bicycle pump

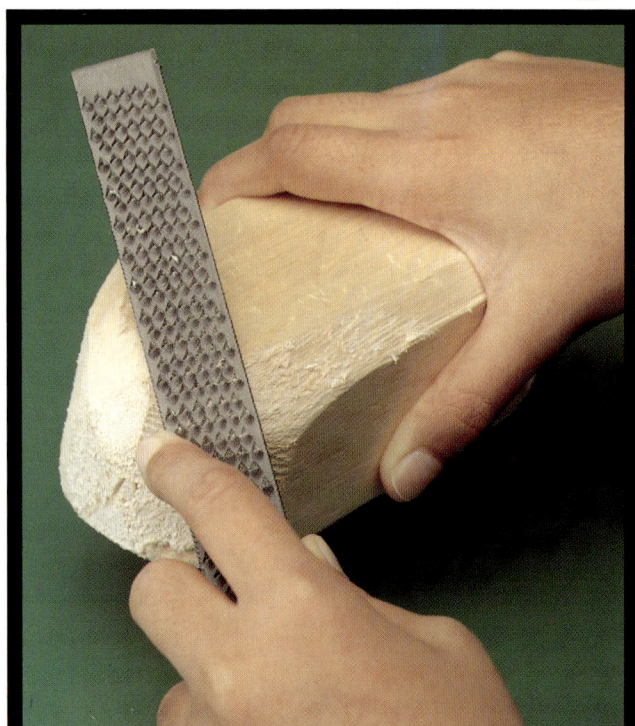

1 Make a hull from balsa wood. Use a rasp and sandpaper to shape the curves.

2 Make a wooden keel shape and fix it to the bottom. Paint the hull and keel with gloss paint or varnish.

3 Cut a triangle of fabric for the sail. Glue or sew it to the mast. Make a hole for the dowel mast and glue the mast into it.

4 Attach the two eye hooks as shown and tie the string to the sail.

5 Test your model in the bath or in a tank of water.

Try setting the sail at different angles.

Can you add a boom of wooden dowel to the bottom of the sail?
Are there any other ways of improving the sail?
Could you make a longer boat with more than one sail?

SAILING Through the Ages

c. 2800 BC
The first sea-going ships were probably sailed by the Chinese or the Egyptians. By 2800 BC, Egyptian sailors were making voyages down the Red Sea and they had crossed the Mediterranean Sea. Chinese records show that their first sea journeys took place at about the same time.

c. 100
Ships called galleys were used by the Egyptians, the Greeks and the Romans (above). They were sleek and fast and were used to ram enemy ships in battle. They were powered by oars. Large galleys had hundreds of oarsmen.

875-985
The Viking longship (above) had a strong keel and could withstand heavy storms. It could also be rowed silently up rivers for surprise attacks. Longships are thought to have been the first ships to cross the Atlantic.

c. 1100
Balsa wood boats have been used for hundreds of years to carry passengers and cargo on Lake Titicaca, high up in the Andes in Peru. These boats were very similar to the early Egyptian boats. The sail was made of reed matting. Balsa boats don't last long because the wood soon becomes waterlogged.

1492
Columbus sailed the *Santa Maria* on his voyage of discovery across the Atlantic. The *Santa Maria* was a carrack, with a crew of about 40 men. The other ships on the expedition were caravels, which were only about 16 metres long.

1498-1499
Vasco da Gama sailed from Europe to India around Africa.

16th century
The galleon (above) developed from the carrack, probably in Spain. The word "galleon" means "great ship". Rows of cannons made the galleons successful and powerful fighting ships in the 16th century.

18th century
In the 18th century, the navies of England, France and Spain sailed heavily armed "men of war". The biggest had crews of 900 men and carried over 100 cannons.

1819
Savannah crossed the Atlantic under sail, assisted by a small steam engine.

1851
The United States' racing schooner, *America,* won the Queen's Cup by beating British yachts in a race in the Solent. The cup is now called the America's Cup. In 1983, an Australian yacht, *Australia II,* won the cup after 100 years of American domination.

1859
The first ironclad warship, the *Gloire,* from France (below) was launched. It had armour plate over a wooden hull.

1912
The *Titanic* made her maiden voyage and struck by iceberg. 1,522 lives were lost.

1915
The liner *Lusitania* was sunk by a German U-boat with the loss of 1,198 lives.

1955
U.S.S. *Nautilus,* the world's first nuclear-powered submarine (above), was launched.

1964
Francis Chichester won the first Observer Single-handed Transatlantic Race in *Gypsy Moth IV.* He went on to become the first man to sail solo around the world.

1866
The fastest sailing ships used for trade were the clippers. They carried cargoes all over the world, and their owners became very wealthy. In 1866, two clippers raced from China to England in just 99 days.

1973-1974
The first Whitbread Round the World Yacht Race was won by *Great Britain II,* captained by Chay Blyth. It took 144 days to cover the 43,000 kilometres. The race takes place every four years.

GLOSSARY

Artifacts Something made by human workmanship, such as pottery, copper dishes, coins etc.

Boom A pole fixed to the bottom of a sail, it helps to stretch the sail.

Bow The front end of the ship or boat.

Bridge The platform on board ship from where the captain gives instructions.

Bullion Large amounts of gold and silver coinage.

Capsize When a boat overturns.

Commerce Trading between nations or individuals.

Excavations To dig and explore a historical site.

Flagship The ship carrying the admiral of the fleet, or flying his flag.

Furl To roll up the sails of a ship.

Galley A ship with both oars and sails.

Hull The main frame, or body, of an ship.

Inshore Operating near to the shore line.

Keel Part of a ship or boat, under the hull.

Knot A nautical mile per hour, the unit of speed measurement at sea.

Maiden voyage The first voyage of a ship.

Manoeuvrable Can be moved into a position needed.

Outboard motor A motor fixed to the outside of a ship or boat.

Quarters The living areas of the crew.

Reef A chain of rocks or coral, near the surface of the water.

Rigging The system of ropes and pulleys used to hoist and support a sail.

Self-righting A boat which rights itself after capsizing.

Silt Fine mud/sand on the sea or river bed.

Stability Being stable, not falling over.

Stern The back end of a ship.

Streamlined Smooth, sleek and offering little resistance to the water.

Submerged Something totally below the water.

Vessel A craft used for transport by water.

RESOURCES

Places to visit

The National Maritime Museum
Park Row
Greenwich
London, SE10
Tel: 081-858 4422

The Cutty Sark Maritime Trust
King William Walk
London, SE10
Tel: 081-853 3589

The Naval Heritage Site
Portsmouth
(includes the *Mary Rose* and *H.M.S. Victory*)

The Shipwreck Heritage Centre
Rock-a-Nore Road
Hastings
East Sussex
Tel: 0424 437452

Royal National Lifeboat Museum
Grand Parade
Eastbourne
East Sussex
Tel: 0323 730717

St. Katharine's Dock
London

Merseyside Maritime Museum
127 Dale Street
Liverpool, O69 3LA
Tel: 051-207 0001

Exeter Maritime Museum
The Haven
Exeter
Devon
Tel: 0392 58075

Useful Addresses

The Director
Royal National Lifeboat Institution
West Quay Road
Poole
Dorset
Tel: 0202 671 133

The *Mary Rose* Trust
College Road
HM Naval Base
Portsmouth
Hants

Many ports and coastal towns have maritime collections. Contact the local tourist board to find out details.

Books to read
Timelines - Ships by Richard Humble. (Watts Books, 1992.)
The Discovery of the Bismarck by Robert Ballard. (Hodder & Stoughton.)
The Discovery of the Titanic by Robert Ballard. (Hodder & Stoughton.)

INDEX

aircraft carrier 5
America's Cup 29
Amoco Cadiz 9, 10
Amsterdam 9, 10

Ballard, Dr Robert 13
balsa wood 28
battleship 5
Birkenhead 9, 11
Bismarck 8, 10
Blyth, Chay 29
bow 7, 30

canoe 17
catamaran 4
Chichester, Francis 29
Clipper 25, 29
Columbus, Christopher 10, 28
Concepcion 9, 11
Cook, James 28

da Gama, Vasco 28

early ships 28
Egyptians 28
emergency equipment 20-21

ferry 4, 6, 21
floating 6-7

galleon 28
galleys 28, 30
Gloire 29
gravity 18
Greeks 28
Gypsy Moth IV 29

Hope 9, 10
hovercraft 5
hull 6, 7, 16, 30

keel 6, 7, 30
Kyrenia 9, 11

lateen sail 24
lifebelt 22-23
lifeboat 16, 17, 19, 20
life-jacket 21
life-raft 20
liner 5
Lusitania 29

Mary Rose 9, 10, 15

navigation 21

oil tanker 4

radar 21
Romans 28

sailing ships 24, 29
sails 24, 25, 26, 27
Santa Maria 9, 10, 28
Santo Antonio di Tanna 9, 11
Savannah 29
schooner 29
Sea Cat 4
shipwrecks 8, 9, 10, 11
sonar 21
speedboat 6
steamships 25
submarine 4

Titanic 8, 10, 12-13, 29

U.S.S. Nautilus 29

Vikings 28

yacht 5, 6, 29

Additional photographs:
Robert Harding Picture Library 13 (© Didier Barrault), 21, 24; Hulton Picture Library 12; Zefa Picture Library 17.